Botanical Beauties
Embroidery

Introduction

Pick up your needle and immerse yourself in the joy of hand embroidery. Whether you're stitching a lush bouquet for your home or adding a personal touch to your daily essentials, these botanical beauties will inspire you to bring the magic of flowers into your life.

The art of embroidery enables you to create pictures with needle and thread. It is an enjoyable pastime, a way to soothe your mind and soul, while bringing beauty to your life. While stitching, you will experience immense satisfaction as images take shape beneath your fingers.

From wall art that will transform any room, to practical yet beautiful accessories, these 8 lovely floral designs can be mastered with the help of our step-by-step instructions and Color/Stitch Guides. Our clear, concise General Instructions aid you in what you need to know about supplies, how to transfer your design to fabric, and how to stitch the design. We include diagrams for a large variety of stitches and instructions for framing your design if desired.

contents

Strawberries

Design by Ria Paramita

The Supplies

Design Size: approximately 5½" (14 cm) diameter

- ☐ 11" x 9 (27.9 cm x 22.9 cm) zippered canvas bag
- ☐ DMC 6-strand embroidery floss — 1 skein each
- ☐ #26 chenille embroidery needle
- ☐ 6" (15.2 cm) diameter wood embroidery hoop
- ☐ Supplies for desired transfer method *(see Transferring Design to Fabric, page 30)*

Refer to the pattern, page 6, and the General Instructions, pages 28-36, to complete your project.

Color/Stitch Guide

DMC	Color Name
700	dark green
989	green
602	dark pink
604	pink
309	red
902	dark red
415	grey
973	yellow
blanc	white

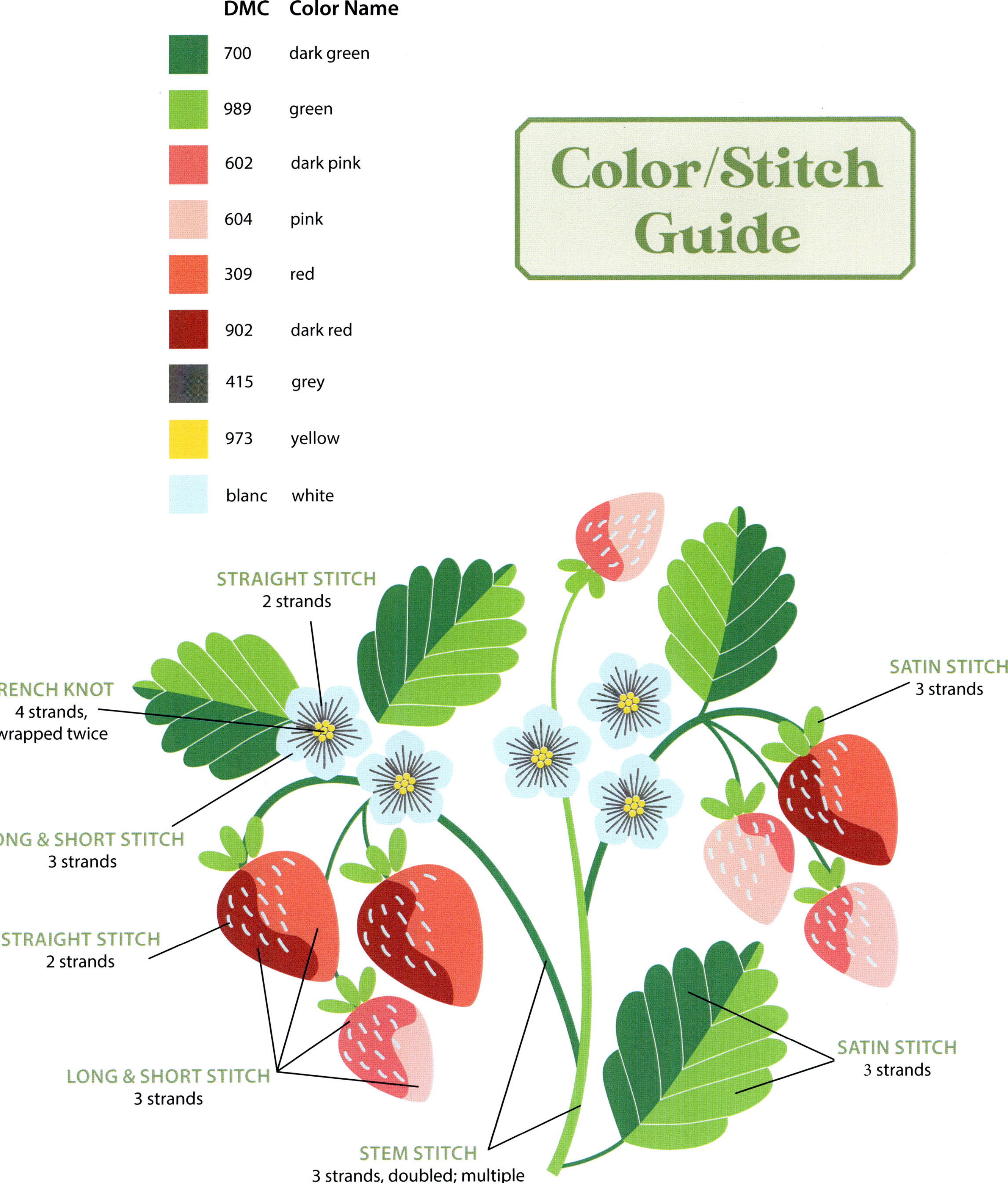

Sunflowers

Design by Ria Paramita

The Supplies

Design Size: approximately 5½" (14 cm) diameter

- ☐ 9" x 9 (22.9 cm x 22.9 cm) piece of cream cotton fabric
- ☐ DMC 6-strand embroidery floss — 1 skein each unless otherwise indicated on Color/Stitch Guide plus 1 yd (0.91 m) to match fabric for finishing back
- ☐ #3 crewel embroidery needle
- ☐ 6" (15.2 cm) diameter wood embroidery hoop
- ☐ Supplies for desired transfer method *(see Transferring Design to Fabric, page 30)*
- ☐ Frame with an approximate 5¾" (14.6 cm) diameter opening

Refer to the pattern, page 9, and the General Instructions, pages 28-36, to complete your project.

	DMC	Color Name
	580	dk green
	166	lt green
	972	dk orange (2 skeins)
	973	yellow (2 skeins)
	433	brown

Color/Stitch Guide

Dahlia

Design by Ria Paramita

The Supplies

Design Size: approximately 5¼" (13.3 cm) diameter

- ☐ 9" x 9 (22.9 cm x 22.9 cm) piece of sheer organza fabric
- ☐ DMC 6-strand embroidery floss —1 skein each unless otherwise indicated on Color/Stitch Guide
- ☐ #3 crewel embroidery needle
- ☐ 6" (15.2 cm) diameter wood embroidery hoop
- ☐ Supplies for desired transfer method *(see Transferring Design to Fabric, page 30)*
- ☐ Craft glue

Refer to the pattern, page 12, and the General Instructions, pages 28-36, to complete your project.

Color/Stitch Guide

DMC	Color Name
353	peach (2 skeins)
3712	coral (2 skeins)
347	dark coral (2 skeins)
347	dark coral
3821	gold
927	light green
931	blue

CHAIN STITCH
3 strands; fill area

For each flower, start with peach petals and make 5 Lazy Daisy Stitches filled with a Straight Stitch. Repeat for coral and dark coral petals – 3 strands

FRENCH KNOTS
Fill area with 3 strands, wrapped twice.

CHAIN STITCH
3 strands

BULLION STITCHES
6 strands
Make 7 Bullion Stitches, wrapping needle 14 times

SATIN STITCH
6 strands

FRENCH KNOTS
3 strands, wrapped twice

STRAIGHT STITCH
3 strands, doubled

Garden Fresh

Design by Ria Paramita

The Supplies

Design Size: approximately 5½" (14 cm) diameter

- ☐ 9" x 9 (22.9 cm x 22.9 cm) piece of cream cotton fabric
- ☐ DMC 6-strand embroidery floss — 1 skein each unless otherwise indicated on Color/Stitch Guide plus 1 yd (0.91 m) to match fabric for finishing back
- ☐ #3 crewel embroidery needle
- ☐ 6" (15.2 cm) diameter wood embroidery hoop
- ☐ Supplies for desired transfer method *(see Transferring Design to Fabric, page 30)*
- ☐ primer, paint and paintbrush

Refer to the pattern, page 15, and the General Instructions, pages 28-36, to complete your project.

Color/Stitch Guide

DMC	Color Name
745	light yellow
3821	yellow
162	light blue
3766	blue (2 skeins)
353	coral
224	light pink
3364	light green
3362	dark green
351	orange

Butterfly Scatter

Design by Ria Paramita

The Supplies

Design Size: approximately 5½" (14 cm) diameter

- ☐ 12" x 12 (30.5 cm x 30.5 cm) white fabric pillow cover
- ☐ DMC 6-strand embroidery floss —1 skein each
- ☐ #26 chenille embroidery needle
- ☐ 6" (15.2 cm) diameter wood embroidery hoop
- ☐ Supplies for desired transfer method *(see Transferring Design to Fabric, page 30)*

Refer to the pattern, page 18, and the General Instructions, pages 28-36, to complete your project.

Color/Stitch Guide

DMC	Color Name
700	green
166	light green
972	yellow
3340	orange
3805	dark pink
605	pink
550	dark purple
553	purple
310	black
ecru	ecru

STEMS AND LEAVES

- Stem Stitch all stems using 4 strands.
- Chain Stitch all leaves using 3 strands.
- Stem Stitch all veins using 3 strands.

BUTTERFLY

- Satin Stitch body using 2 strands.
- For wings, Satin Stitch outer edges and Split Stitch veins using 2 strands. Use Long and Short Stitch to fill wings using 2 strands. Use French Knots for spots using 2 strands, wrapped once.
- Straight Stitch antennae using 1 strand.

Clover

Design by Ria Paramita

The Supplies

Design Size: approximately 5" (12.7 cm) diameter

- ☐ 9" x 9 (22.9 cm x 22.9 cm) piece of beige cotton fabric
- ☐ DMC 6-strand embroidery floss — 1 skein each plus 1 yd (0.91 m) to match fabric for finishing back
- ☐ #3 crewel embroidery needle
- ☐ 6" (15.2 cm) diameter wood embroidery hoop
- ☐ Supplies for desired transfer method *(see Transferring Design to Fabric, page 30)*
- ☐ Frame with an approximately 5¾" (14.6 cm) diameter opening
- ☐ Primer, paint, and paintbrush

Refer to the pattern, page 21, and the General Instructions, pages 28-36, to complete your project.

Color/Stitch Guide

DMC	Color Name
902	dark pink
223	pink
225	light pink
08	brown
500	dark green
3363	green
3022	light green
ecru	ecru

LEAF DETAILS

- Stitch ecru leaf veins.
- Beginning at top center, stitch top section of leaf.
- Stitching from side to center, stitch bottom of leaf in 2 sections.

Blessed

Design by Laura Gushue

The Supplies

Design Size: approximately 5¼" (13.3 cm) diameter

- ☐ 9" x 9 (22.9 cm x 22.9 cm) piece of cream cotton fabric
- ☐ DMC 6-strand embroidery floss —1 skein each unless otherwise indicated on Color/Stitch Guide
- ☐ #3 crewel embroidery needle
- ☐ 6" (15.2 cm) diameter wood embroidery hoop
- ☐ Supplies for desired transfer method *(see Transferring Design to Fabric, page 30)*
- ☐ Frame with an approximate 5¾" (14.6 cm) diameter opening

Refer to the pattern, page 24, and the General Instructions, pages 28-36, to complete your project.

Color/Stitch Guide

DMC	Color Name
blanc	white (3 skeins)
371	light green
3787	green
844	gray
839	brown
3768	blue
3773	peach

Work light green French Knots around leaves & flowers using 6 strands.

SPLIT STITCH
3 strands

BACKSTITCH
3 strands

BLESSED

SPLIT STITCH
3 strands

FRENCH KNOT
6 strands

SATIN STITCH
6 strands

WOVEN WHEEL STITCH
6 strands (doubled)

STRAIGHT STITCH
6 strands

LAZY DAISY STITCH
6 strands

BLESSED

Growing Flowers

Design by Michal Loren

The Supplies

Design Size: approximately 5½" (14 cm) diameter

- ☐ Tote bag with fabric pocket — our bag is 12¾" x 12¼" (32.4 cm x 31.1 cm) with an 11⅝" x 9" (29.5 cm x 22.9 cm) pocket
- ☐ DMC 6-strand embroidery floss — 1 skein each
- ☐ 6" (15.2 cm) diameter wood embroidery hoop
- ☐ #26 chenille embroidery needle
- ☐ Supplies for desired transfer method *(see Transferring Design to Fabric, page 30)*

Refer to the pattern, page 27, and the General Instructions, pages 28-36, to complete your project.

Color/Stitch Guide

DMC	Color Name
349	red
3713	pink
718	fuchsia
554	lavender
680	gold
3813	light green
890	dark green

Use 2 or 3 strands of floss as indicated for stitches.

- Use Straight Stitch (2 strands) to stitch inside of flowers.
- Use Stem Stitch to outline each flower and flower center (2 strands).
- Add French Knots (2 strands), wrapping needle twice.
- Use Straight Stitch (3 strands) for long flower stems.
- Use Lazy Daisy Stitch (3 strands) for remaining flower centers and leaves.

General Instructions

Before you begin, read through the following pages to familiarize yourself with the tools and supplies you will be using. Try your hand at making The Stitches, pages 34-35, on a scrap piece of fabric.

Supplies

Fabric

Our framed designs feature either white, cream, or a slightly rough-textured ecru lightweight cotton fabric. If you are just learning how to embroider, a fabric with a fairly dense weave will give you the best result.

The Dahlia design, page 10, is embroidered on sheer organza. Organza is a sheer lightweight fabric. Due to it's light weight, transparent nature it is slightly more difficult to embroider on and more difficult to hide your thread ends. To hide the ends, trim the thread ends close to the knot. Use small dabs of glue to glue the ends behind the areas of stitching. The finished result is stunning!

Floss

All the projects in this book use DMC 6-strand embroidery floss. It is inexpensive and easy to work with and comes in a huge variety of colors from which to choose.

Needles

Needles are a very personal choice. We used a size 3 crewel embroidery needle for all lightweight cotton fabrics and a #26 chenille embroidery needle for heavier fabrics such as canvas. Embroidery needles have long, oval eyes and sharp points for piercing the fabric. Look for needles that have eyes large enough to accommodate the number of strands or size thread you will be using without making excessively large holes in the fabric. Try different sizes of needles until you find one that suits you.

Hoops

A 6" (15.2 cm) hoop will be used for embroidering the design and sometimes for finishing the completed project. It is important to keep the fabric stretched taut while embroidering so your stitches will look uniform and the fabric will remain free from puckers. The fabric is placed over the inner ring and the outer ring is tightened over the fabric with a screw-type tension adjuster to hold the fabric taut. A variety of hoops are available in various sizes and materials, such as wood or plastic. Many embroiders prefer wood hoops and a wooden hoop will be needed if the project is being finished in the hoop. Removing the hoop after each stitching session will keep your fabric free from permanent creases and indentations.

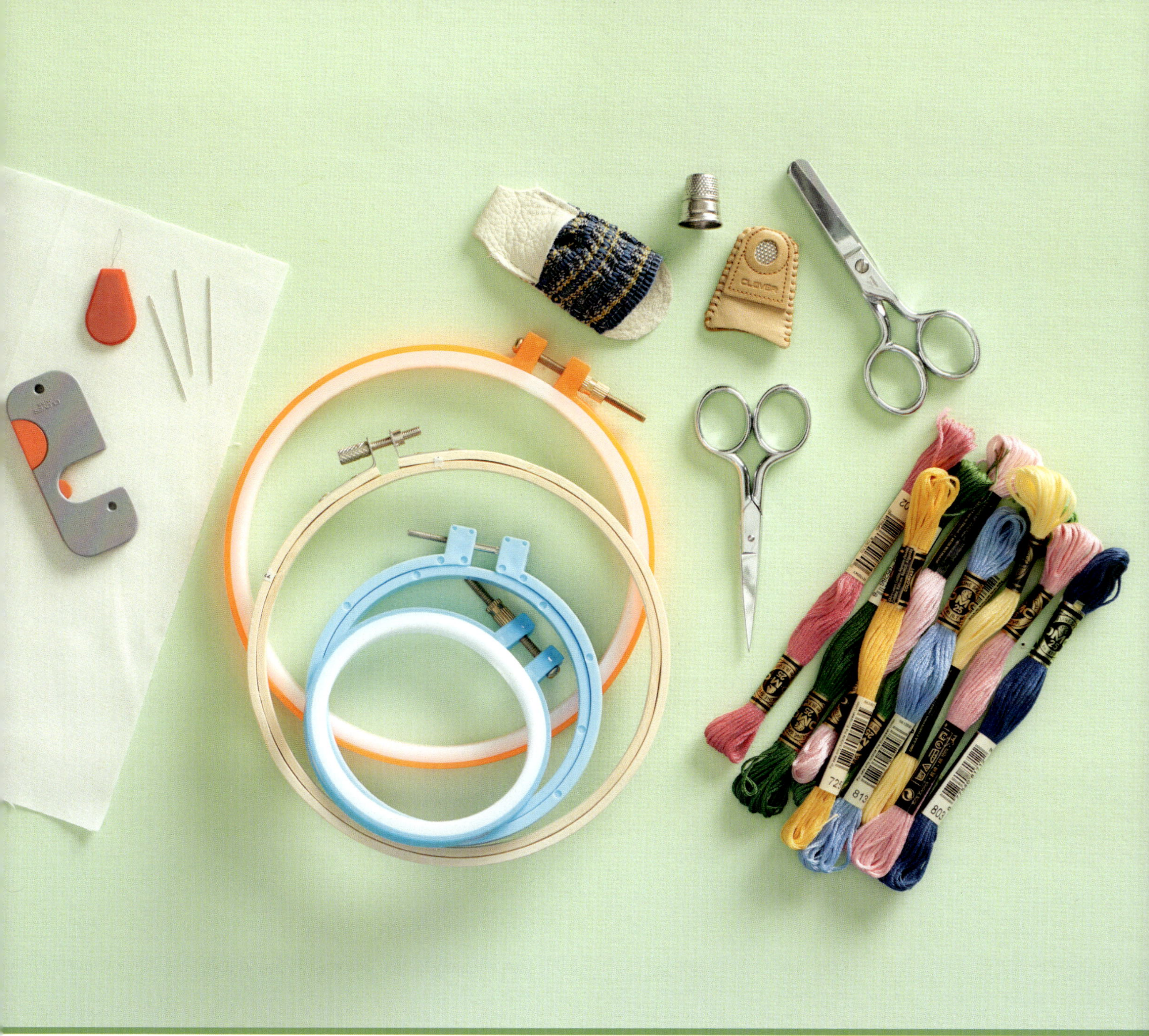

Other Tools

A needle threader comes in handy when using multiple strands of floss.

A thimble protects the middle fingertip while embroidering. Some embroiderers wouldn't stitch without one, while others find them distracting. Experiment to see if a thimble is right for you, and give yourself time to adjust to it.

Small, sharp embroidery scissors clip thread and floss quickly and neatly. The pointed tips can be used for pulling out any unwanted stitches. Reserve your scissors only for embroidery so they stay clean and sharp. Protect the points (and your finger!) by storing the scissors in a sheath.

Transferring Design to Fabric

There are various ways to transfer designs from the book to fabric. Choose one of the following methods. The method you choose may depend on the item to which you're transferring.

Direct Tracing

- fine-point water-soluble pen
- tape
- light source

This method allows you to trace directly onto the fabric. Tape the fabric piece over the pattern and trace the design with a fine-point water-soluble pen. If you have trouble seeing through the fabric, you can make a photocopy of the pattern, tape the pattern on a light box or light pad, tape the fabric over the pattern, and trace the design. You can also tape the pattern to a sunny window, tape the fabric over the copy, and trace the design. Embroider the design.

Freezer Paper Tracing

- freezer paper [8½" x 11" (21.6 cm x 27.9 cm) sheets]
- copier/printer
- light source
- fine-point water-soluble pen

The freezer paper method stabilizes the fabric pieces which makes tracing easier. Using the mirror image function on a copier, copy the pattern onto the paper side of freezer paper. With shiny side down, iron the freezer paper to the wrong side of your fabric piece. Using a light box, or light pad, or sunny window, trace the design with a fine-point water-soluble pen. Remove freezer paper before embroidering. This method is helpful when transferring the pattern to organza. Embroider the design.

Transfer Paper

- tissue paper
- wax-free transfer paper
- fine-point water-soluble pen

Trace the pattern onto tissue paper. Place the transfer paper, colored side down, between the fabric and the pattern. Use a pen to draw over the traced pattern. Embroider the design. This method is helpful when transferring the pattern to the pillow or bags.

Sticky Water-Soluble Paper Stabilizer

- sticky water-soluble paper stabilizer
- ink jet printer

This stabilizer is a pliable film through which you can embroider. Follow the manufacturer's instructions to photocopy the design onto the "film" side of a sheet using the light setting on your ink jet printer. Remove the paper backing and adhere the pattern to the right side of the fabric. Embroider the design. Trim the excess film away from the embroidery. Soak the fabric in cold water to dissolve the film.

Embroidering the Design

1. Loosen the turn screw on the top of the hoop and separate the hoop pieces. Center the design, right side up, on the inner hoop. Place the outer hoop over the fabric and inner hoop and tighten the turn screw. Gently pull the fabric evenly around the edges until the fabric is tight in the hoop. It will be easier to embroider if the fabric is stretched tightly in the hoop.

2. The floss colors we used are listed in the Color/Stitch Guide with the DMC color number and color name. Each floss color can be stitched with 1 floss skein or less unless otherwise indicated. Decide where you would like to begin embroidering. Refer to the Color/Stitch Guide to determine the floss color, how many strands to use, and the stitch to be used. Cut an 18"-24" (45.7 cm - 61 cm) floss length. Longer lengths tend to twist, look worn, and knot more easily. Separate the floss length into six separate strands. To separate, hold the floss at one end and "fan out" the individual strands; select one end and pull it out. Straighten the remaining floss after each separation. Repeat to separate each strand. Align the ends of the required number of strands and lay them parallel to one another. Handling them as one, thread the needle. Tie a knot close to the long end of the floss.

3. Begin with an away waste knot. From the front, take the threaded needle down into the fabric 3"-4" (7.6 cm x 10.2 cm) from where you choose to begin embroidering. The knot will be trimmed off later and the floss ends woven under stitches. Referring to The Stitches, pages 34-35, embroider the chosen area. When you finish embroidering that area or run out of floss, run the needle under some nearby stitches to anchor the floss. Trim the floss close to the embroidered piece. Strive for consistent tension as you work.

4. Continue to embroider in this manner until you have completed the design. Reposition the fabric in the hoop as necessary. After you have a good bit stitched, carefully trim the away waste knot from the fabric, pull the floss ends to the wrong side and run the end under stitches. You may not need to use an away waste knot every time you start a new floss length. You can run the new floss length under existing stitches.

5. If you used direct tracing or freezer paper tracing, remove any visible marks with a damp cotton swab. If you used sticky water-soluble paper stabilizer, follow manufacturer's instructions to remove film.

The Stitches

Always come up at 1 and all odd numbers and go down at 2 and all even numbers, unless shown otherwise.

BACK STITCH

Fig. 1

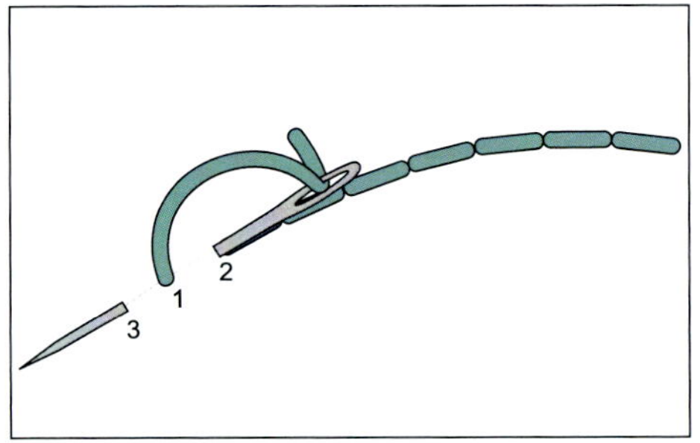

BULLION STITCH

Come up at 1, go down at 2, and come up again at 1; don't pull needle through fabric. Wrap needle 14 times ***(Fig. 2A)***. Pull needle through wraps ***(Fig. 2B)*** and pull taut against fabric ***(Fig. 2C)***. Use needle to settle wraps in place. Go down again at 2 to secure stitch ***(Fig. 2D)***.

Fig. 2A

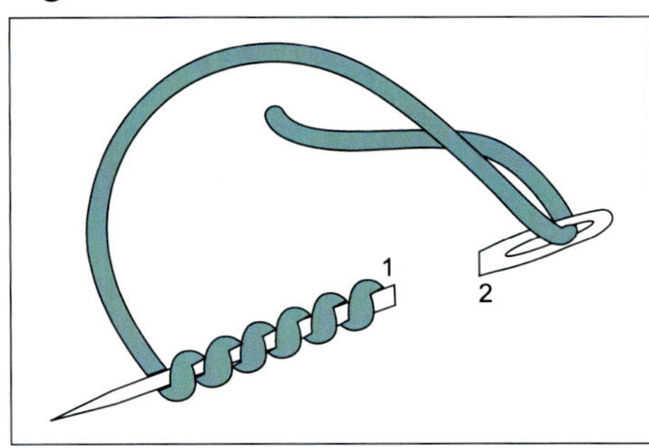

Fig. 2B

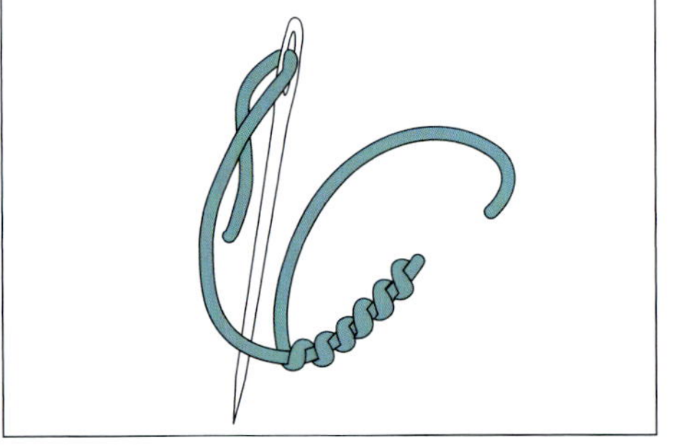

Fig. 2C

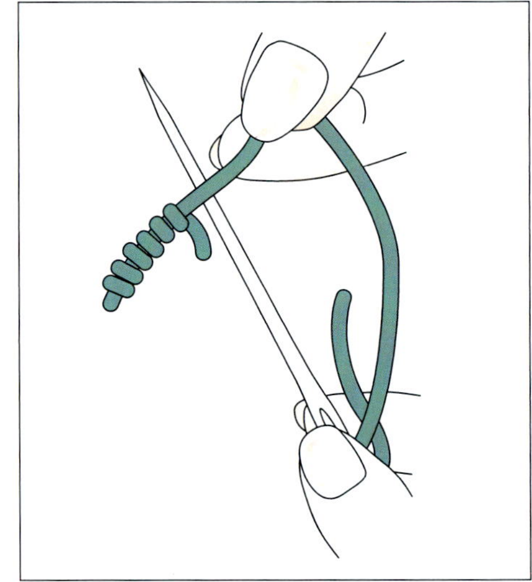

Fig. 2D

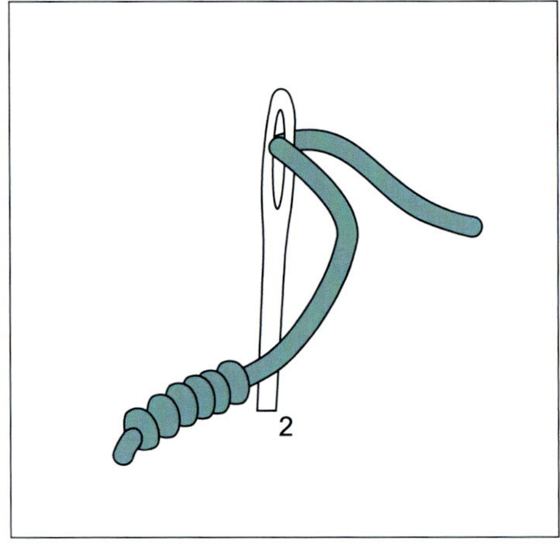

CHAIN STITCH

Fig. 3

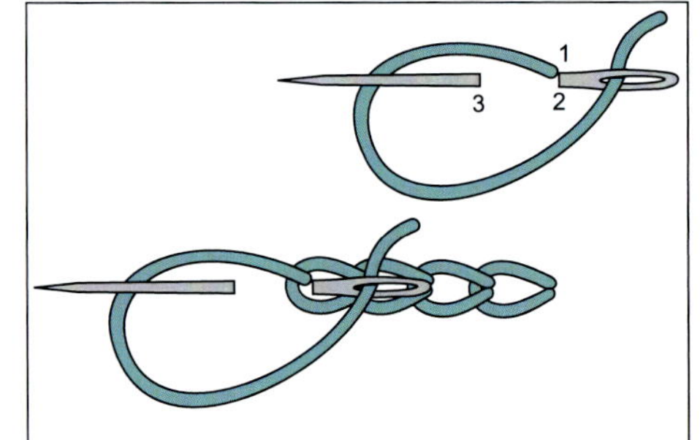

CLOVER STITCH

Using light pink, stitch 6 horizontal lines across clover. Bring the needle up from the wrong side of the fabric in the center below thread 2. Loosely wrap floss 4-5 times over threads 1 & 2. Repeat to stitch on each side of this stitch on threads 2 & 3. Changing floss colors as needed and wrapping stitches as shown, continue stitching over horizontal threads. Bring needle to wrong side of fabric; tie off.

Fig. 4

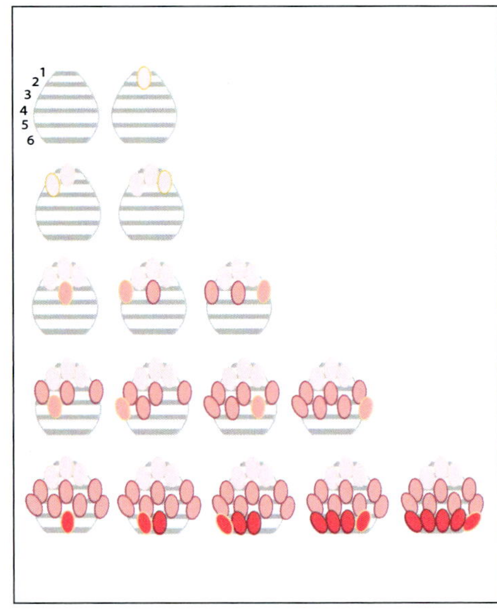

FRENCH KNOT

Fig. 5

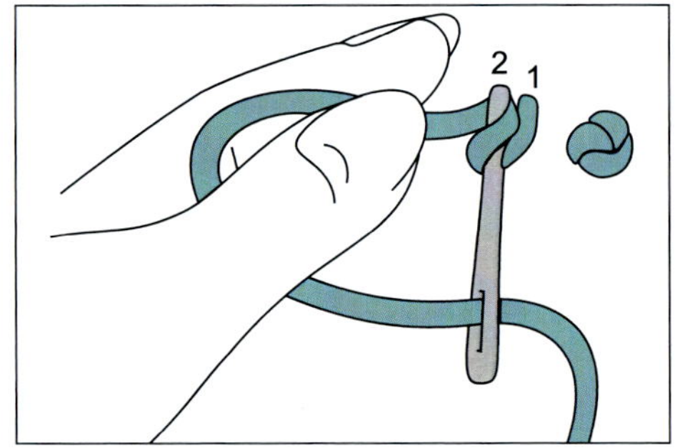

LAZY DAISY STITCH

Fig. 6

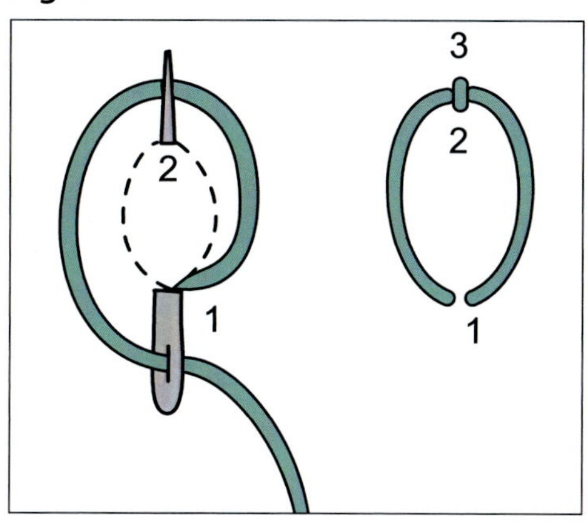

LONG & SHORT STITCH

Fig. 7A

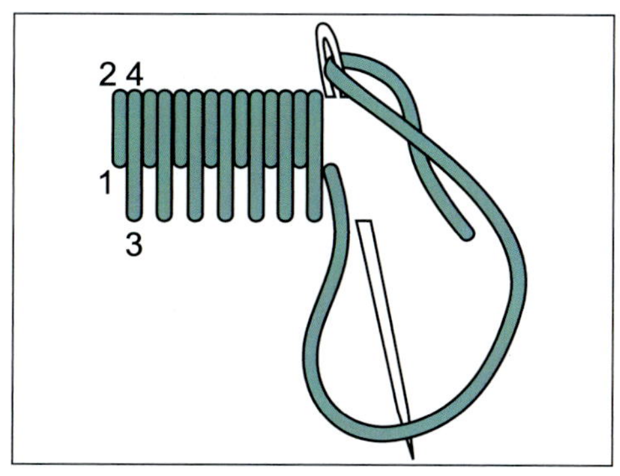

Fig. 7B

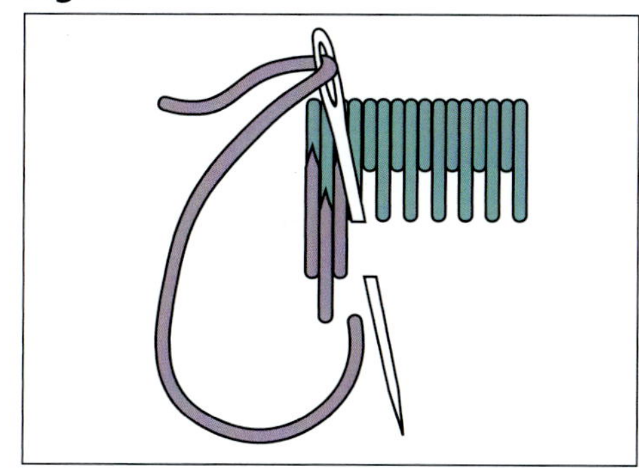

Fig. 7C

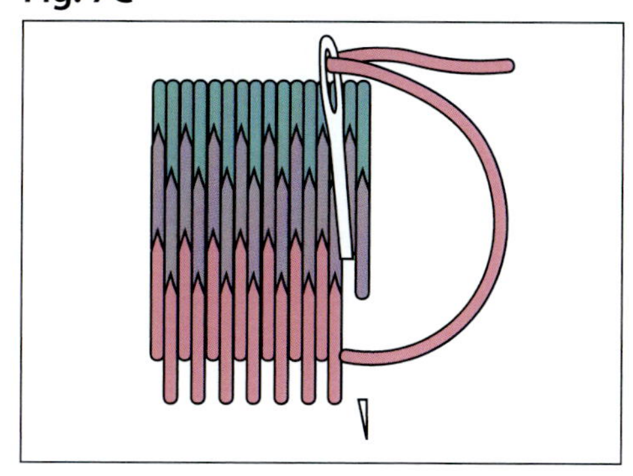

RUNNING STITCH

Fig. 8

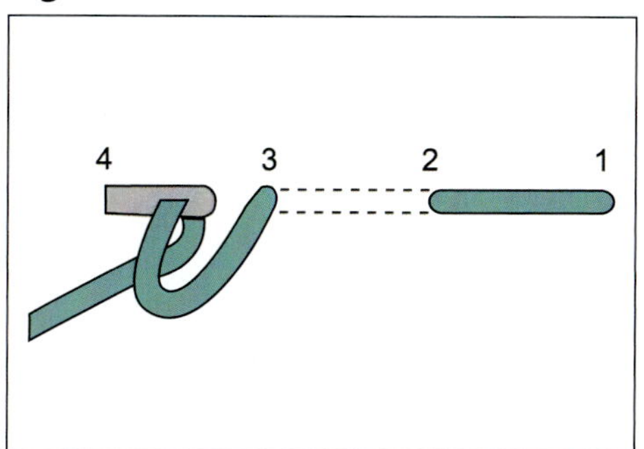

SATIN STITCH

Fig. 9

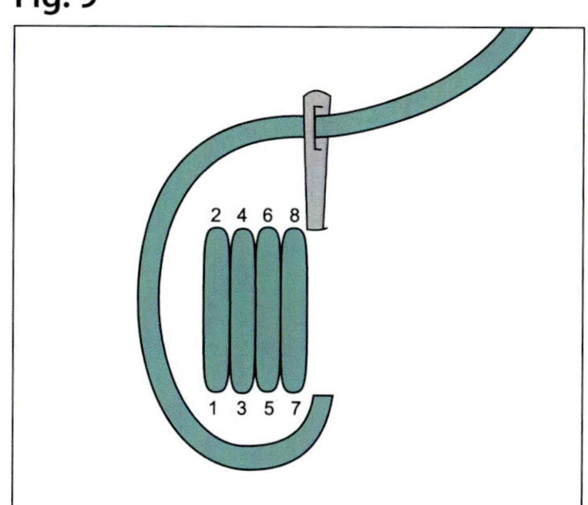

SPLIT STITCH

Fig. 10

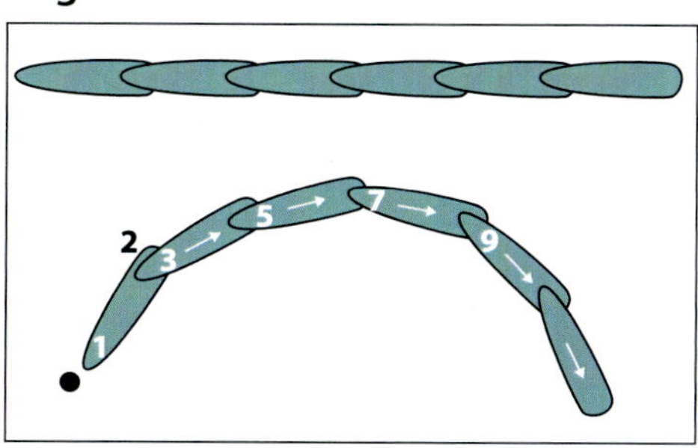

STEM STITCH

Fig. 11

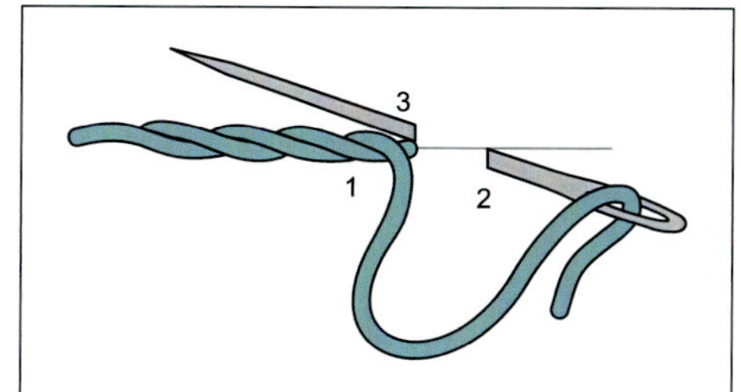

STRAIGHT STITCH

Fig. 12

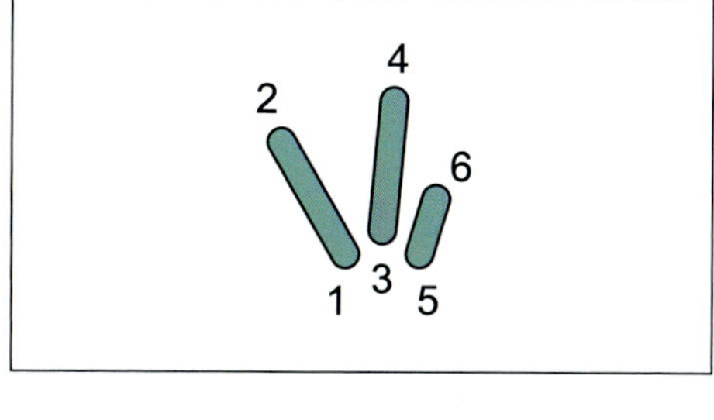

WOVEN WHEEL

Fig. 13A

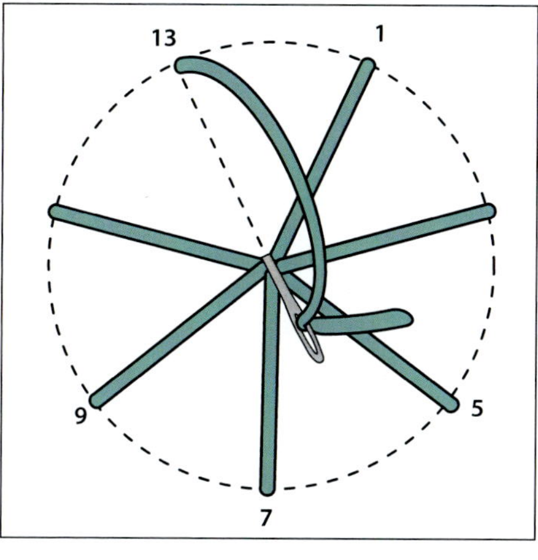

Fig. 13B

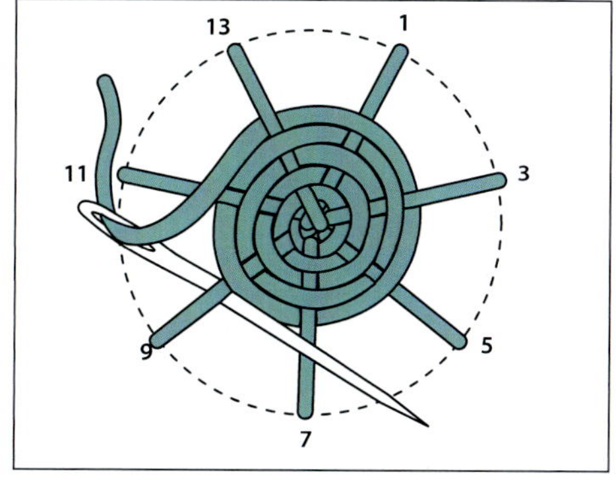

WEAVING

Fig. 14

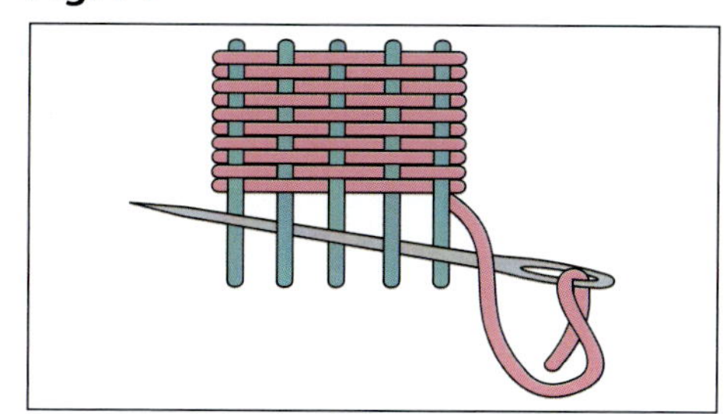

Framing

Your completed design can be mounted and framed in the same embroidery hoop in which it was stitched.

1. If using cotton fabric, recenter and tightly secure the design in the hoop. Trim the fabric to about 1½" (4 cm) beyond the hoop edge. Using floss that matches the fabric, work Running Stitches about ½" (1.3 cm) from the cut edge; do not trim the floss ends. Pull the floss ends to gather the fabric. Tightly knot the floss ends together and trim any excess.

   If using organza, recenter and tightly secure the design in the hoop. Trim the fabric close to the hoop edge. Paint a bit of craft glue over the cut fabric edges and on the embroidery hoop; let dry.

2. We choose to paint the outside ring of our hoop as shown on Garden Fresh, page 13. We simply painted the outer hoop with acrylic paint, being careful not to get paint on the metal parts. Allow to dry thoroughly before replacing outer ring on completed design.

   We used embroidery hoop display frames with approximately 5¾" (14.6 cm) openings to frame many of our designs. With these frames, your completed design will slide into the back of the frame and is held in place with elastic. These wood-tone frames can be used as is or they can be primed and painted using acrylic paint in any color you choose.

Production Team: Technical Editor - Lisa Lancaster; Technical Associate Editor - Mary Sullivan Hutcheson; Graphic Artist - Christine Roa DeLillo; Photo Stylist and Photographer - Rob Karman.

Made in U.S.A.